Thomas Edison

To Ryan Yamato Kolentsi, who also lights up the world— E.M.

For Monika and Jogi, with love— A.K.

Kids Can Read ® Kids Can Read is a registered trademark of Kids Can Press Ltd.

Text © 2008 Elizabeth MacLeod
Illustrations © 2008 Andrej Krystoforski

Kids Can Press gratefully acknowledges the financial support of the Government of Ontario, through the Ontario Media Development Corporation; the Ontario Arts Council; the Canada Council for the Arts; and the Government of Canada, through the CBF, for our publishing activity.

Published in Canada and the U.S. by Kids Can Press Ltd.
25 Dockside Drive, Toronto, ON M5A 0B5

Kids Can Press is a Corus Entertainment Inc. company

www.kidscanpress.com

Edited by David MacDonald
Designed by Marie Bartholomew

Educational consultant: Maureen Skinner Weiner, United Synagogue Day School, Willowdale, Ontario.

This book is perfect bound.

Library and Archives Canada Cataloguing in Publication

MacLeod, Elizabeth
    Thomas Edison / written by Elizabeth MacLeod ; illustrated by Andrej Krystoforski.

(Kids Can read)
ISBN 978-1-55453-058-8

1. Edison, Thomas A. (Thomas Alva), 1847–1931—Juvenile literature.
2. Inventors—United States—Biography—Juvenile literature. 3. Electric engineers—United States—Biography—Juvenile literature. I. Krystoforski, Andrej, 1943– II. Title. III. Series: Kids Can read (Toronto, Ont.)

TK140.E3M33 2008   j621.3092   C2007-906549-X

Thomas Edison

Written by Elizabeth MacLeod
Illustrated by Andrej Krystoforski

Kids Can Press

Click! With a flip of a switch, you flick on a lamp. It shines brightly, thanks to the light bulb inside it.

Your world would be much darker without light bulbs. Thomas Edison created this great invention. He invented many other things, too.

Thomas Alva Edison was born in 1847 in Ohio, in the United States. His family called him Al.

Al asked lots of questions when he was a little boy. He wanted to find out how things worked.

When Al was two years old, he saw a mother goose sitting on eggs in her nest. He knew this made the eggs hatch.

Al wondered if eggs would hatch if *he* sat on them. His parents pulled him off before he could find out.

Al watched candles and oil lamps glow. He was curious about fire. When he was six, he decided to learn more about it. He lit a fire in his family's barn.

This was a dangerous thing to do. Soon the whole barn was on fire! Al got out just in time.

Next, Al was curious about how birds fly. He saw them eat worms. Did that help birds fly?

Al mushed up worms with water. Then he asked a friend to try the drink. That was not a good idea. She got very sick!

When Al was about 12, he got a job working on railroad trains. He sold fruit, candy, postcards and newspapers.

Al had a lot of free time while he was on the train. So he set up a lab in the train car that held the baggage.

One day, Al was doing an experiment when the train rocked. Al's lab equipment went flying and started a fire. No one was hurt, but Al could no longer have a lab on the train.

Next, Al decided to write a newspaper to sell on the train. People liked Al's paper and he sold many copies.

By the time Al turned 15 in 1862, he had chosen a new name. Now he wanted to be called Tom.

Later that year, Tom was waiting at a train station. A little boy named Jimmie was playing on the tracks.

Suddenly, Tom saw a train car rolling toward Jimmie. Tom raced over and pushed him out of the way. Thanks to Tom, Jimmie was safe.

Jimmie's father had no money to give Tom to thank him. Instead, he taught Tom how to use a telegraph machine.

At the time, the telegraph was the fastest way to send messages over long distances. The machine used a special code called Morse code.

Tom learned the code and became very fast at sending telegraph messages. For the next six years, he traveled around Canada and the United States. Tom worked in many telegraph offices.

In 1869, Tom arrived in New York City, New York. He began working for a company that made telegraph equipment.

Tom came up with an idea for making telegraph equipment work better. His idea was so good that the company paid him lots of money.

Tom opened a workshop. There, he could invent and build his machines.

Whenever he could, Tom spent time in his workshop. Even on the day he got married in 1871, Tom worked on one of his inventions.

Tom hired lots of people to help him in his workshop. He expected everyone to work hard. But Tom liked to have fun, too. He often played jokes on the people who worked for him.

Tom was not like most bosses. He did not always dress neatly. Sometimes he took quick naps in the workshop. If Tom was working hard, he did not stop for dinner until midnight.

In 1876, Tom moved his workshop to Menlo Park, New Jersey. The next year, he invented a special pen.

When people wrote with this pen, it pricked tiny holes in the paper. Then people could press ink through the holes to quickly make copies.

That same year, Tom invented the first machine that could record sounds and play them back.

Tom called his invention a phonograph (FONE-o-graf). This machine could play music, like a CD player, but it used tubes instead of discs.

Tom was inventing more than 130 years ago. Back then, people used candles, oil lamps or gas lamps to light their homes.

These lights could be smoky and could also start fires. Tom wanted to make a light that used clean, safe electricity.

To create light from electricity, Tom needed to make a light bulb. He put two wires to carry electricity inside the bulb. Between the wires was a thin thread.

When electricity flowed along the wires and thread, the thread heated up. That made it glow.

But the thread in the light bulb burned up too fast. The bulb quickly went dark.

For more than a year, Tom worked on the light bulb. He tried making the thread from many things, such as hair and wood.

Nothing worked. But Tom did not give up.

In the fall of 1879, Tom tried making the thread out of cotton that had been baked in an oven. This light bulb stayed lit for more than thirteen hours.

Tom's light bulb was a success!

Tom wanted to show people his new light bulb. He planned a special party for New Year's Eve.

First, Tom set up lots of light bulbs in his workshop. Then he put lights in other houses in the town. Some of his lights were strung up on poles outside.

On New Year's Eve, hundreds of people waited in the streets of Menlo Park. When Tom flipped a switch, all the light bulbs lit up. The crowds were amazed.

In 1887, Tom moved into a new lab in West Orange, New Jersey. This lab was ten times bigger than his last workshop.

There, Tom invented the movie camera. The movies it filmed were very short. Some were just 16 seconds long! But people learned how to make longer movies.

In 1909, Tom invented a very strong battery. It could power electric cars.

Between 1914 and 1918, many countries were fighting in a war. Tom invented ways to find enemy planes and submarines.

Tom became very rich. But he loved working and never stopped. During his life, Tom created more than 1000 inventions. No one has ever invented more.

Tom died when he was 84. On the day of his funeral, people across the United States turned off their lights for one minute.

When people turned their lights back on, they remembered Tom. He was the inventor who lit up the world!

More facts about Tom

- Tom was born on February 11, 1847. He died on October 18, 1931.

- When Tom was young, he began to have trouble hearing. Later, he became almost completely deaf.

- You can visit Tom's homes in West Orange, New Jersey, and in Fort Myers, Florida. At Menlo Park, New Jersey, there is a museum about Tom's inventions.

- Tom's favorite invention was the phonograph.